Creative Life Publishing & Learning Institute
www.CLPLI.com
Info@CLPLI.com

Book Versions
Ingram Spark Paperback ISBN: 978-1-946265-40-1

Copyright © 2022 Shirley J. Fink

All rights reserved. No part of this book may be reproduced in any form without prior written permission from the publisher. This work represents the views and opinions of the author alone. No liability in conjunction with the content or the use of ideas connected with this work is assumed by the publisher.

THE HOLY BIBLE, NEW INTERNATIONAL VERSION®, NIV® Copyright © 1973, 1978, 1984, 2011 by Biblica, Inc.® Used by permission. All rights reserved worldwide.

"New International Version" and "NIV" are registered trademarks of Biblica, Inc.®.

My Day Begins with Jesus

MATT. 1:21

I dedicate this book to my daughter, Patricia Andreassen, who encouraged me to write it.

A portion of the proceeds of "My Day Begins With Jesus" goes to the Church of God Orphanage based out of Cleveland, TN.

To schedule Shirley to bring her message and singing to your church please email publishing@clpli.com.

ABOUT SHIRLEY J. FINK

I was brought up in a Christian home. At a very young age I joined the Oliver Ave. Church of God in Princeton, West Virginia.

I married Carl Fink at the age of 18 years old. He was in the US Navy in San Diego, California. When I moved to San Diego, we went to the Church of God.

I became involved in the church. I taught the Sunday School Bible class, played the piano for the choir and preached there also. I worked in church work since a child. At my age, I still have the desire to be a blessing to someone.

No matter how old or how young you are you can make a difference in someone else's life.

I was saved in a Methodist Church in Brush Fork, West Virginia when I was about 10 years old, sanctified and filled with the Holy Ghost.

My Dad was a minister, and we helped him in the ministry, sang and played music in the church.

I am 85 years old, and I am praying this book will inspire you today. My aim is to point you to Jesus. If you don't know Him, or if you have strayed away from Him please call now and put your trust in Him today.

Great things will begin to happen in your life. It's never too late. Just believe.

Rev. Shirley J. Fink
Licensed with Church of God, Cleveland, Tennessee
www.RevShirleyFink.com

The angel of the Lord encamps around those who fear him, and he delivers them. - Psalm 34:7

Now there is in store for me the crown of righteousness, which the Lord, the righteous Judge, will award to me on that day—and not only to me, but also to all who have longed for his appearing.
- 2 Timothy 4:8

When I was a child growing up
in Brushfork, W.VA.
A child at the Methodist church.
In A.Revival. The minister showed the
painting of Christ crucified on the cross.
The alter filled up with young people
that day.
I gave my heart to Jesus. And wrote
this poem.
                                        S.J.F.

HE DIED FOR ME

Verse 1
I saw a beautiful picture
of Jesus, my Lord one day.
He showed me that He died for me,
and then I began to pray.

Verse 2
The soldiers drove nails, thru His hands,
and also thru His feet.
They pierced the Saviour in his side
they wanted Jesus to die.

Chorus
Someday He's coming back again,
to take His children away.
To a wonderful beautiful mansion
forever in Heaven to stay.

Verse 3
He prayed to his Heavenly Father,
forgive them, for what they do.
And this is the way that Jesus
on the cross, gave His life for you.

Verse 4
They did not know, He could arise,
and go to Heaven above.
He arose and ascended on a cloud
more beautiful than a dove.

-Words and music by Shirely Fink

Teach me your way, Lord; lead me in a straight path because of my oppressors. - Psalm 27:11

Be kind and compassionate to one another, forgiving each other, just as in Christ God forgave you. - Ephesians 4:32

Watch The Butterfly

I saw Two Butterflies This MORNING,
Floating Around on A Bush Nearby
It Taught me that Nothing really matters
Keep Looking to Heaven on High.

You See, Your DAYS Are ALL Numbered,
God mAde ALL Things PLeasant For Thee,
though You wALk The VALLey BeFore you
You smeLL The Roses So sweet.

You'LL FLy Like The Butterfly greatly-
For Heaven Someday you wiLL See
Get Not engrosed with EARTLy things
But Cheerful As the ButterFLy Agrees.

Keep Yourself As A spiritual Being,
Float Around As A Butterfly goes
You're Looking To Find The Right Answer.
It's in Jesus, Our Saviour. You Know.

S.J.F.

He saw that there was no one, he was appalled that there was no one to intervene; so his own arm achieved salvation for him, and his own righteousness sustained him. - Isaiah 59:16

Blessed are the meek,
for they will inherit the earth. - Matthew 5:5

Blessed are the merciful,
for they will be shown mercy. - Matthew 5:7

Blessed are the peacemakers,
for they will be called children of God. - Matthew 5:9

Blessed are those who are persecuted because of righteousness, for theirs is the kingdom of heaven. - Matthew 5:10

Blessed are the pure in heart,
for they will see God. - Matthew 5:8

Words And Music By: Shirley Jean Fink

He's Alive Oh Praise His Name

①
The disciples gathered Near - To hear the words of Christ, so dear,
I must die upon the Cross of Calvary
For the Sins of All Mankind, That I might Live A Life Sublime.
I must Die, But Live Again - Eternally.

CHORUS
He's Alive - Oh, Praise His Name
The Tomb is empty, He's Not here, His spirit Reigns.
He's Coming Back - He's Coming Soon,
Keep your hearts in Tune with God - Not Filled with gloom.

②
A betray'l of Kiss That Day - Took my Lord And Christ Away.
The Jews Then Mocked And Scorned Him, Don't you see.
This was Ordained To Be: To set the Captive Free -
Now All who Come to Christ, Have Victory -

③
As They Laid Him in a tomb. Sadness filled Their hearts with gloom
Understanding Not His Death, Nor soon Return.
He Arose The Third Day, Conquered Death, Hell, And The grave.
He's Alive And Lives Forever - Praise His Name.

© Copyright Broadriver Publishing - All rights Reserved
Shirley Fink

Blessed are those who mourn,
for they will be comforted. - Matthew 5:4

Blessed are those who hunger and thirst for righteousness, for they will be filled. - Matthew 5:6

Blessed are you when people insult you, persecute you and falsely say all kinds of evil against you because of me. - Matthew 5:11

Sing to him a new song;
play skillfully, and shout for joy. - Psalms 33:3

BROAD RIVER COLLECTION, TRIBUTE AND PRAISE – 2001

Verse 1
Make me a blessing, dear Lord I pray.
Guide and direct me along life's dark way.
Shield and protect me from evil and strife,
show me thy glory throughout my whole life.
When I'm in danger, thy sword will I yield.
Sanctify Holy, my sweet life to shield.
You are my Savior, my soon coming King.
Glory and honor and praise.

Chorus
Glory and honor and praise to the King,
Master of glory, His praises I'll sing.
Teach me to trust and obey thy great word
Father of mercy and master of love.
Sounds of bells ringing in heaven above.
Draws me much closer to redeeming love.
You are my master, the hope of my life,
Glory and honor and praise.

Verse 2
This world with it's sadness, the trouble and woe.
Words of the master, get ready to go.
A home is now waiting for you and for me,
those who are blood bought thru Calvary.
Cleanse me and mold me and make me a light.
Shining in darkness through out the dark night.
You're my mediator, my anser to prayer.
Glory and honor and praise.

Repeat chorus and end.

Trust in the Lord and do good;
dwell in the land and enjoy safe pasture. - Psalms 37:3

That person is like a tree planted by streams of water, which yields its fruit in season and whose leaf does not wither— whatever they do prospers. - Psalms 1:3

For God so loved the world that he gave his one and only Son, that whoever believes in him shall not perish but have eternal life.
- John 3:16

For God so loved the world that he gave his one and only Son, that whoever believes in him shall not perish but have eternal life.
- John 3:16

But the gift is not like the trespass. For if the many died by the trespass of the one man, how much more did God's grace and the gift that came by the grace of the one man, Jesus Christ, overflow to the many! - Romans 5:15

I delight greatly in the Lord; my soul rejoices in my God.
For he has clothed me with garments of salvation and arrayed me in a robe of his righteousness, as a bridegroom adorns his head like a priest, and as a bride adorns herself with her jewels.
- Isaiah 61:10

Therefore, my dear brothers and sisters, stand firm. Let nothing move you. Always give yourselves fully to the work of the Lord, because you know that your labor in the Lord is not in vain. - 1 Corinthians 15:58

Keep yourselves in God's love as you wait for the mercy of our Lord Jesus Christ to bring you to eternal life. - Jude 1:21

Therefore, since we are surrounded by such a great cloud of witnesses, let us throw off everything that hinders and the sin that so easily entangles. And let us run with perseverance the race marked out for us. - Hebrews 12:1

Learning to Lean

I sought you with tears, Dear Father,
I felt you was so far away.
But then I began to wonder.
He walks with me every day.

You told me you'd never leave me
So finally I began to believe
For Faith cometh by Hearing
The words that my Lord did relieve

So when you are down and discouraged,
Be thankful you are alive.
To pray and trust in the Saviour
Who maketh you brightly shine.

This world has it's trouble and heartaches,
Don't wrestle your thoughts in despair
But remember the words of Jesus.
Just Lean on me every hour.

Dear Friend, Don't look on the dark side.
The Spirit within you doe'th glow,
The Faith in you is much greater.
The things that you never will know.

Cheer up, find hope in tomorrow
And ALL Things will FLOURISH AND GROW.
TAKE Time to TALK To the Saviour
Your sins will Become Whiter Than Snow.

                                              S.J.F.

But the eyes of the Lord are on those who fear him,
on those whose hope is in his unfailing love. - Psalms 33:18

Nevertheless, God's solid foundation stands firm, sealed with this inscription: "The Lord knows those who are his," and, "Everyone who confesses the name of the Lord must turn away from wickedness."
- 2 Timothy 2:19

Whoever has ears, let them hear. - Matthew 11:15

Then those who feared the Lord talked with each other, and the Lord listened and heard. A scroll of remembrance was written in his presence concerning those who feared the Lord and honored his name. - Malachi 3:16

I am a rose of Sharon, a lily of the valleys. - Song of Solomon 2:1

But now, Lord, what do I look for? My hope is in you
- Psalms 39:7

CARRY ME BACK

Song written by Rev. Shirley J. Fink
July 25, 2022

Verse 1
I lived in the hills of West Virginia
In a country so brave and so kind,
Where we all gathered around the table
All nine of use, happy with smiles.

Chores
So carry me back to West Virgina,
To the mountain that I love the best.
Where the trees are all swaying with gladness
With the thoughts of my Mother and Dad.

Verse 2
The birds sweetly singing each morning
And the rivers are flowing with smiles.
No time for a heart to be broken
Just wake up, smell the roses incline.

Verse 3
I could hear the panthers calling at mid-day.
Where the gardens of vegetables lay,
My Mom cooked the best golden breakfast,
I'll never forget that great day.

Verse 4
Since childhood I sang and played music,
I could hear the birds chirping at times.
The orchard all grew full with apples,
Dad picked the black berries from the vine.

People will dwell again in his shade; they will flourish like the grain, they will blossom like the vine—Israel's fame will be like the wine of Lebanon. - Hosea 14:7

But love your enemies, do good to them, and lend to them without expecting to get anything back. Then your reward will be great, and you will be children of the Most High, because he is kind to the ungrateful and wicked. - Luke 6:35

We wait in hope for the Lord; he is our help and our shield. - Psalms 33:20

For God so loved the world that he gave his one and only Son, that whoever believes in him shall not perish but have eternal life.
- John 3:16

The life of mortals is like grass, they flourish like a flower of the field;
- Psalms 103:15

When the TERRORIST ATTACK happened, I WAS At my FRIEND house.
   I Ask God To give me A song on the TERRORIST ATTACK.
   IT ALL cAme into my heArt And I wrote Down The Words.

                                   S.J.F.

OUR NATION, USA

Words & music By
Rev. SHirley J. Fink
9/20/01

© Copyright - All Rights Reserved. 2001
Brood River Publishing Co.

①

Our Country And our Nation
All in one Accord doeth stand.
For The Terrorist And Hijackers
Have Attacked our Lovely Land
We Are Firm And Faithful in Belief
As Uniform we stand
Victory is just Ahead.

(2)

We will be overcomers
Of the land and on the sea.
Our Nation is equipped with force
Against the enemy
We'll attack if necessary
The opposers of Liberty.
God's Glory doeth prevail

(3)

We Are a God fearing Nation,
And we know no defeat,
We have warred and kept our Nation
Under Air and ship And feet.
For forever we are Greatful.
And we know no fear nor foe.
Victory in God - We know.

CHORUS

Hallulujah, what a Nation.
And United we do stand,
The United States of America.
Keeps Their word And Never fails

She will give birth to a son, and you are to give him the name Jesus,[a] because he will save his people from their sins.
- Matthew 1:21

Therefore, since we have been justified through faith, we[a] have peace with God through our Lord Jesus Christ,
- Romans 5:1

Repent, then, and turn to God, so that your sins may be wiped out,
that times of refreshing may come from the Lord,
- Acts 3:19

Not only so, but we[a] also glory in our sufferings, because we know that suffering produces perseverance;
- Romans 5:3

"The Spiritual MAN"

It came into my spirit about the scripture Ps 1:3 "Blessed is the MAN."

He is like a tree planted by the river of water that bringeth forth his fruit in the season. His leaf shall not wither and whatsoever he doeth shall prosper.

What kind of a tree are you?

There are many trees bearing fruit.

Compared to a tree, what fruit are you bearing?

The fruit of the Spirit is love, joy, peace, longsuffering, gentleness, kindness, goodness, peace and self control.

If you, as a tree, are not flourishing you are withering away.

But to be fresh and anointed, you must bear fruit on thy tree, good fruit and fresh leaves.

God is the vine and you are the branches. John 15:5

When Jesus was with his deseiples and came to a fig tree which had no figs. He said "No fruit on thee forever" The fruit tree withered away.

Will Jesus on the last day, see you as a fruit bearing tree and say "Good and Faithful Servant, Enter into the joys of the Lord," or will he say "I never knew you."

Come back to God, fertilize your tree, and make fruit again. Matt. 12:33

S.J.F.

There is a time for everything, and a season for every activity under the heavens: - Ecclesiastes 3:1

Sing the praises of the Lord, you his faithful people;
praise his holy name. - Psalms 30:4

I will sing the Lord's praise, for he has been good to me.
- Psalms 13:6

Do your best to present yourself to God as one approved, a worker who does not need to be ashamed and who correctly handles the word of truth. - 2 Timothy 2:15

Consecrate yourselves and be holy, because I am the Lord your God.
- Leviticus 20:7

From the fruit of their lips people are filled with good things,
and the work of their hands brings them reward. - Proverbs 12:14

THE STORY OF THE BIG BUG AND SMALL ANT

I sat on the front porch this morning to feel the wind and watch the cars to by – I saw a big bug and a small ant on the concreate, crossing to the other side.

The big bug was slow and very determined. The ant, though small, attached the big bug on each side.

The big but, very determined, told the ant "get away right now." This did not change the ants mind. He continued to hassle the bug.

After ten minutes, the ant gave up and ran away.

The journey for the big bug, though slowly making his way, accomplished his task.

"So friends"

Keep going, don't give up. Your journey will be completed.

Satan is defeated for you succeeded in "peace."

For God so loved the world that he gave his one and only Son, that whoever believes in him shall not perish but have eternal life.
- John 3:16

May I never boast except in the cross of our Lord Jesus Christ, through which[a] the world has been crucified to me, and I to the world.
- Galatians 6:14

my God is my rock, in whom I take refuge, my shield and the horn of my salvation. He is my stronghold, my refuge and my savior—
from violent people you save me.
- 2 Samuel 22:3

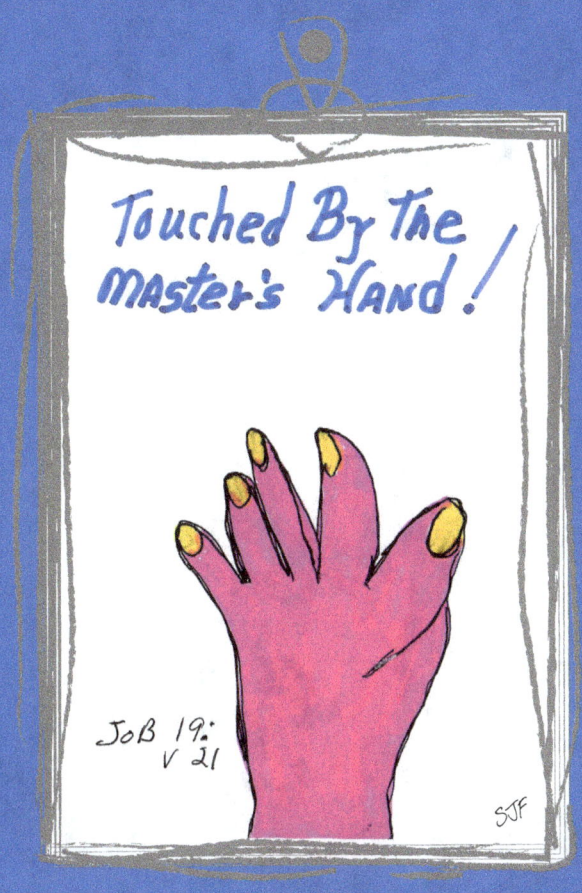

Have pity on me, my friends, have pity, for the hand of God has struck me. - Proverbs Job 19:21

So you also must be ready, because the Son of Man will come at an hour when you do not expect him. - Matthew 24:44

What's Ahead

Ye know not what's on the Schedule,
That God has prepared for you.
Just wake up and face it with gladness
And happy, its made up for you.

Ye know not what's on tomorrow,
Today is a glittering view
You find it in God's perspective
Don't rush, just stay in God's truth.

He promised the day would be brighter
If only you trust and obey.
For sometimes we get off the pathway.
And end up in trouble, dismay.

So cheer up and look to the Father
Please help me to know the right way-
So here I am dear Father.
Please guide me each moment, each day.

Thanks always for all you have done
My victory in Christ has been won.
No matter what befalls me today.
Thanks again for showing me the way

S.J.F.

The Lord makes firm the steps of the one who delights in him;
- Psalms 37:23

If any of you lacks wisdom, you should ask God, who gives generously to all without finding fault, and it will be given to you.
- James 1:5

"Have faith in God," Jesus answered. - Mark 11:22

www.ingramcontent.com/pod-product-compliance
Lightning Source LLC
Chambersburg PA
CBHW052122110526
44592CB00013B/1711